# DREAMS OF LEAVING

Also by David Hare

PLENTY
FANSHEN
TEETH 'N' SMILES
KNUCKLE
SLAG
LICKING HITLER

with *Howard Brenton*
BRASSNECK (Methuen)

# Dreams of Leaving

A film for television by
DAVID HARE

FABER & FABER
London          Boston

First published in 1980
by Faber and Faber Limited
3 Queen Square London WC1N 3AU
Typeset by An Grianán
Printed in Great Britain by
Lowe and Brydone Printers Limited
Thetford Norfolk
All rights reserved

All rights whatsoever in this play are strictly reserved
and applications for permission to perform it must be
made in advance, before rehearsals begin, to Margaret
Ramsay Ltd, 14a Goodwin's Court, St Martin's Lane,
London WC2

British Library Cataloguing in Publication Data

Hare, David
Dreams of Leaving
I.  Title
822'.9'14        PR6058.A678D/

ISBN 0-571-11568-3

for DARCY

# CHARACTERS

WILLIAM
CAROLINE
ANDREW
STIEVEL
XAN
STONE
COLIN
AARON
MRS ALEXANDER
ROBERT
KEITH
Lawyers, Journalists, Waiters, Dancers,
Secretaries, Girlfriends, Boyfriends, etc.

*Dreams of Leaving* was first shown on BBC TV in January 1980. The cast was as follows:

| | |
|---|---|
| WILLIAM | Bill Nighy |
| ANDREW | Andrew Seear |
| STIEVEL | Johnny Shannon |
| COLIN | Charles Dance |
| AARON | Julian Littman |
| CAROLINE | Kate Nelligan |
| STONE | Tony Matthews |
| KEITH'S LAWYER | Raymond Brody |
| KEITH | Gary Holton |
| XAN | Mel Smith |
| AN OLDER JOURNALIST | David Ryall |
| MISS COLLINS | Annie Hayes |
| ROBERT | Hilton Macrae |
| MINISTER | Peter Williams |
| MRS ALEXANDER | Helen Lindsay |
| DOCTOR | George Raistrick |
| LAURA | Maria Harper |

| | |
|---|---|
| *Photography* | Mike Williams |
| *Producer* | David Rose |
| *Director* | David Hare |

## 1. EXT. ENGLISH COUNTRYSIDE. DAY

*The English countryside. Green hills, cows, trees. Then suddenly, without warning, rushing through frame, a British Rail inter-city train hurtling along unseen rails. It passes. We look at the empty track.*

[*Then the words:*]
'Dreams of Leaving'

[*Then WILLIAM'S voice:*]
WILLIAM: [*V.O.*] I first came to London in 1971.

## 2. INT. TRAIN. DAY

*An open carriage, every seat taken. WILLIAM coming down the aisle of the train looking for a seat. He is scruffily dressed in a corduroy suit with a white mackintosh which he wears throughout the film. He has one large suitcase and carries eight newspapers. He is from Nottingham. He is twenty-four, tall, attractive, badly turned-out.*

WILLIAM: [*V.O.*] Time of course has cemented things over, so this now seems like the inevitable course. But at the time I had no idea what I was doing. I didn't know if it was breakfast or lunch.

## 3. EXT. EARLHAM STREET. DAY

*WILLIAM coming out of the door of his new flat and walking along the pavement. Behind him, the Victorian façade of a red-brick central London block, in one of the small streets off Cambridge Circus. It has a warehouse on the ground floor; then, above that, we see the arched windows of a tiny group of small flats.*

WILLIAM: [*V.O.*] I pretty soon found a place where I could live and at the beginning girls were easy to meet...

## 4. INT. CINEMA. NIGHT

*WILLIAM sitting alone in the cinema. One seat away is an AMERICAN GIRL, heavy with denim. She is big-boned, dark-haired, about twenty-one, also sitting alone.*

WILLIAM: [*V.O.*] Perhaps the only time in my life that's been true.
   [*An extract from the film he is watching:* Duel in the Sun. *Jennifer Jones runs to the cell door to plead for a stay in her father's execution.*]
   I even picked a girl up at the cinema, something I wouldn't even contemplate now.

11

## 5.   INT. WILLIAM'S ROOM. NIGHT

*The room is very small and looks like a student's bedsitter. An old armchair, a bed, a messy roll-top desk. Little effort to decorate: some magazine pictures on the wall and a couple of prints. An old black-and-white television. WILLIAM and the AMERICAN GIRL lying in bed together.*

GIRL: All right?

WILLIAM: What? [*Pause*] Yes. Yes I'm fine.

## 6.   INT. WILLIAM'S FLAT, KITCHEN. NIGHT

*WILLIAM's view of the AMERICAN GIRL's back as she stands talking at the stove wearing only a miniskirt and a feather boa round her neck. With one hand she is scrambling eggs, with the other she is drinking gin. WILLIAM sits at a small table by the wall. He looks subdued.*

WILLIAM: [*V.O.*] Everyone says Americans are obsessed with hygiene, but it never seemed to interest the ones I met.

## 7.   EXT. FLEET STREET. DAY

*A large newspaper office seen from the outside. A great black building. Then, once it's established, WILLIAM running at high speed out the door to catch a passing bus.*

WILLIAM: [*V.O.*] I managed at last to get a job round the time I was living with someone called Angela, or thought I was, because she was never there...

## 8.   INT. WILLIAM'S FLAT, STAIRS. NIGHT

*WILLIAM hastening up the brown-painted stairway to his flat.*

WILLIAM: [*V.O.*] It was six days before I realized she'd left me and another six before I could get over it.

## 9.   INT. FLATS. ANDREW'S ROOM. NIGHT

*The door of ANDREW's room opening as WILLIAM leans in from the corridor. It is identical to WILLIAM's in shape, but it is tidy and painted white. Bookcase, scrubbed wooden table where ANDREW now sits working under an Anglepoise, his books and papers stacked around him. He is the same age as WILLIAM, very quiet and dry. A naturally grave and decent man.*

WILLIAM: Angela not here?

ANDREW: No.

## 10.   INT. WILLIAM's ROOM. NIGHT

*WILLIAM coming into his own room. He turns the light on and stands at the door. The eiderdown is on the floor, the clothes are all over.*

WILLIAM: [*V.O.*] Part of me knew she was with someone else and part of me wouldn't admit it because...no let's stick to what I have to say.

12

## 11. INT. NEWSPAPER OFFICES. NIGHT

*STIEVEL in a huge open-plan office. At once the phone rings. At once he picks it up.*

STIEVEL: Night desk. [*Pause. He makes notes.*] Yeah. [*Pause*] Yeah absolutely. Don't worry, Lonnie, the whole thing's in hand.

[*WILLIAM has arrived and is standing holding some grubby sheets of paper as STIEVEL puts the phone down and spikes his notes. He is about fifty, very casual in shirtsleeves, with very thick pebble glasses. Behind him the huge newsroom stretches away, now quiet. The pooling of the light makes it emptiness very beautiful.*]

WILLIAM: Somebody left me this stuff to go over.

STIEVEL: Okay, sure, let me take a look. [*He takes the paper, looks at his watch.*] Did you get time off for supper?

[*WILLIAM shakes his head. STIEVEL reaches for the bottle of whisky on top of his desk.*] Here. Help yourself. Have some of mine.

[*WILLIAM takes it and drinks as STIEVEL checks through the copy. WILLIAM looks across to the far entrance, some thirty feet away, where CAROLINE and AARON are now standing. She is thin, dark-haired, good-looking, about twenty-four, smart and easy in boots and a loose dress, unmistakably from classless London; as it proves, Notting Hill. She is much taller than AARON who is only five foot, with long black hair, like a decadent schoolboy. He seems about eighteen, but is really twenty-five, and Cockney. STIEVEL, oblivious, checks through, emphasizing certain words.*]

STIEVEL: Senior government ministers *assembled*...it was beer and sandwiches for lunch...

[*WILLIAM watches as, from his desk on the other side of the room, COLIN gets up to greet the strangers at the door.*]

COLIN: Ah, can I help you? Are you who I'm waiting for? [*He is in his mid-thirties, very posh, with squashed features and crinkly hair.*] My name is Colin. I write the gossip. [*He smiles.*] Don't worry, it's all right, I shan't gossip about you.

[*AARON has already taken something from his pocket and now palms it across to COLIN.*]

COLIN: Are you going to tell me where it comes from?

AARON: No.

COLIN: Okay.

AARON: I mean...

COLIN: No. Fair enough. [*He stands a moment.*] Well look. All right? I hope you'll excuse me. I'd be grateful...I'll just take a look. [*He goes and sits at the nearest desk, swings the Anglepoise round, unwraps the tinfoil and examines his small lump of hash. STIEVEL's voice meanwhile.*]

STIEVEL: Talks in *deadlock*...nation held to *ransom*...old women
   dying in the *street*...
   [*WILLIAM watches as CAROLINE and AARON talk very
   quietly together as they wait, an odd pair.*]
AARON: You hungry? [*CAROLINE nods.*] Go and eat pasta?
CAROLINE: Yes I'd like to.
AARON: I'm very hot on clams.
   [*COLIN gets up, as if at Sotheby's.*]
COLIN: This looks first-rate. I have to thank you. It's such a bitch
   getting decent stuff around here. I don't suppose you have any-
   thing harder...
AARON: We have laughing gas. But only in cylinders.
COLIN: Yes. [*Pause*] Well perhaps not. Why don't I...
AARON: Pay?
   [*COLIN gestures to the door, as he gets out his wallet. But
   CAROLINE is staring straight across at WILLIAM, her gaze
   absolutely level at thirty feet. She stares.*]
COLIN: Are you coming...
CAROLINE: Caroline. [*Pause*] Yes. I'm coming. [*But she still
   doesn't move. She just stands, staring at WILLIAM, and then
   suddenly turns lightly to COLIN, and they go.*] How do you
   choose who to persecute?
COLIN: What?
CAROLINE: On the column?
COLIN: Oh well...I mean...
   [*WILLIAM's view of their backs as they disappear through the
   distant door.*]
   I don't think we'd call what we do persecution; I've always
   believed the public has a right to know...
   [*They've gone. WILLIAM turns back.*]
WILLIAM: Well? What d'you think? D'you think I should cut it?
STIEVEL: It's fine. It's absolute rubbish. [*He smiles.*] Congratul-
   ations. You have the house style.


## 12. EXT. STREET. NIGHT

*A single lamp-post throwing its light through the London drizzle on
to the pavement. WILLIAM passing on his way home. A pause. We
look at the empty street, then WILLIAM's voice.*
WILLIAM: [*V.O.*] From that day on things were never easy. Something had changed...for the rest of my life.


## 13. INT. WILLIAM'S ROOM. NIGHT

*WILLIAM sitting in the old armchair opposite ANDREW who is
stretched out on the bed. They both have glasses of beer. WILLIAM
has just answered the phone.*
WILLIAM: Meryl. God. Hey. Good to hear you. Yeah, I meant to.
   Well, how are you? [*He looks straight at ANDREW.*] Fact is it's

14

ridiculous, I'm in bed with measles. Andrew leaves my medecine outside the door. [*Pause*] No... [*Pause*] No I know... [*Pause*] Well you know I would like that. [*He has picked up what is obviously her very intimate tone.*] Sure. [*Pause*] I know... [*Pause*] That would be very good. [*He laughs a little.*] Yeah well...yeah...yeah...lovely... [*Pause*] Look why don't I send you my stuff in a bottle? That would be something. Wouldn't it? D'you think? [*Pause. The tone changes.*] No, no, I promise I was joking... [*Pause*] No, well sometimes I can't tell myself. [*Pause*] Of course. No, well look... [*Pause. Then very cold.*] I'll talk to you Meryl. [*The phone being put down at the other end. WILLIAM holds the receiver away from his ear, looks straight at ANDREW.*] Shameless. [*Pause*] Ugly. [*Pause. He laughs.*] Absurd.

## 14.  EXT. EARLHAM STREET. NIGHT
*Seen from across the street, the lights in WILLIAM's flat going out one by one.*
WILLIAM: [*V.O.*] I thought I could begin to clear up the shambles, I had the idea of sorting out my life.

## 15.  INT. GALLERY. PUBLIC ROOM. DAY
*WILLIAM standing alone in a white space. He has plastered down his hair, put on a clean shirt and tie, gestured towards cleaning his raincoat. He stands, notebook in hand. Then after a few seconds, CAROLINE arrives, friendly, in a white blouse and full skirt.*
CAROLINE: Are you the journalist?
WILLIAM: Yeah I'm William Cofax. I rang you earlier. It's good of you to meet.
CAROLINE: You must tell me...
WILLIAM: I just want some background.
CAROLINE: Yes. I'm sure. Let me do what I can.

## 16.  INT. GALLERY. PUBLIC ROOM. DAY
*They stroll together through the large white room. Behind them are highly-coloured abstracts on the wall. There is an empty desk, like a receptionist's, at which CAROLINE works.*
CAROLINE: This is really just the façade of the gallery. This is where anyone can come in off the street. We have the usual changing exhibitions; they're regularly advertised, anyone can come. [*She stops and looks round the whole room.*] It isn't really the centre of the business. The real selling...well...that goes on elsewhere.

## 17. INT. GALLERY. VIEWING ROOM. DAY
*The door being opened on a small room, formally laid out. It is heavily curtained in velvet, artificially lit and no more than twelve-*

*foot square: like a plush cell. At one end there is an easel, now*
*empty. At the other three chairs, that's all.*
CAROLINE: You see. In here. This is where it happens. This is
   where they do nine-tenths of their trade. [*She has moved into*
   *the room and stands by the easel. WILLIAM stays near the*
   *door. She gestures at the easel, then at the chair dead opposite*
   *it.*] The customer sits down. He's alone with the painting. [*She*
   *smiles slightly.*] Once he sits down it takes nerve to get up.

18. INT. GALLERY STORE. DAY
*The store: a large room lined with shelves and canvasses which are*
*all stacked away on rails. CAROLINE and WILLIAM walk picking*
*their way round the sculptures, which are lying around, labelled, on*
*the floor. The paintings are mostly hidden till you pull them out on*
*rails. CAROLINE and WILLIAM coming down the centre, talking.*
CAROLINE: These are the bins. Mostly they hold this stuff, release
   it on the market at a certain rate. The idea is to protect any
   artist they sell. Too much of an artist's work comes available
   and you pretty soon find his price starts to slide. [*She smiles.*]
   Who wants to pay top price for a Picasso when there are
   twenty other Picassos for sale? [*She stops by the racks.*] So
   we keep an eye on all the other outlets, buy everything up and
   hold it in here. [*She points to a sculpture WILLIAM is walking*
   *round.*] Moore. [*Another.*] Hepworth. [*She pulls out a canvas*
   *on a long rail, disappearing behind it.*] Mondrian. [*WILLIAM*
   *pulls one out. She comes beside him to look at it.*] That's a
   Rothko. [*She considers it a moment.*] They sort of float in
   space. [*We look at it. CAROLINE's voice meanwhile.*] That's
   why the galleries prefer dead artists. They don't spoil the
   market by turning out more.

19. INT. GALLERY STORE. DAY
*Later. WILLIAM pulls out the largest canvas of all. A man being*
*sick in the lavatory.*
WILLIAM: What sort of price do people charge for a Bacon?
CAROLINE: Well it entirely depends on the size. When we can get
   hold of one we look in the price book, there's a charge per
   square foot; we take a tape measure, work it out like that.
WILLIAM: But that's...
CAROLINE: What?
WILLIAM: Doesn't quality come into it?
CAROLINE: Of course not. Why should it? That's not our job.
   [*She slides the Bacon back.*]
WILLIAM: But if Bacon painted a masterpiece, wouldn't they feel
   that they had to charge more?
CAROLINE: Good Lord no, what, hell are you mad? [*She smiles.*]
   Then when he did a bad one, they'd have to charge less.

16

## 20. INT. GALLERY. DAY

*Later. They walk together along an open space, paintings all turned to the wall.*

WILLIAM: Something about it...it's really amazing...

CAROLINE: It's just logical. It's a business, that's all. [*They walk. He looks around, lost for something to say.*] I can tell it must hurt your ethics. Ethics mean so much in Fleet Street, I know. [*They smile.*]

WILLIAM: All right.

CAROLINE: Well...

WILLIAM: Would you come to dinner?
    [*She stops, turns and looks at him.*]

CAROLINE: Why do you find it so hard to ask?

## 21. INT. GALLERY OFFICES. DAY

*WILLIAM standing uneasily in the corridor outside some smart offices in the gallery. He is waiting. The door is slightly ajar. Away to the back of the offices by a window is a languid, dark-haired man of about forty, with his feet on the desk, talking into a phone.*

STONE: I tell you what I'm thinking. Let's dump the Hockney. I don't see why we shouldn't. It's easy to unload. [*Pause*] Two men. That's right. Having a shower. [*Pause*] How should I know? Shampoo? Could be soap.
    [*CAROLINE passes across the room with a few letters in her hand. She stands in front of a desk which we cannot see, handing them across one by one.*]

CAROLINE: Can I leave you these? I'll be back in the morning...

STONE: Tell you what, I'll throw in the etchings, call it a series then you're away...

CAROLINE: This is for Stone when he's ready to sign. [*She hands the last one across.*] I'm going out.

SECRETARY'S VOICE: Are you going out with the journalist?
    [*A slight pause.*] Why don't you ask him if he's got a friend?
    [*CAROLINE smiles, not knowing she's observed, an absolutely private smile, and turns back across the room, moving out of shot. STONE's voice rising insistently at the back.*]

STONE: Our attitude is this: it's a figurative masterpiece and if he doesn't like it let him shit in his hat.

## 22. INT. GALLERY OFFICE. DAY

*CAROLINE coming out into the corridor, smiling, fresh.*

CAROLINE: Where we going, William?

WILLIAM: Oh what...well...I was thinking... [*They stand.*] Well to be honest...I was hoping you'd say.

## 23. EXT. GALLERY. DAY

*WILLIAM's and CAROLINE's backs as they leave the gallery.*

*talking together.*

WILLIAM: [*V.O.*] I realize now from the beginning...I was never
myself when I was with her. [*His hand, just failing to touch her
back, as they leave.*]

## 24.  INT. WILLIAM'S ROOM. NIGHT

*WILLIAM opening the door of the room. It has been transformed.
The lights are already on. For the first time it is tidy and covered
with greenery, hanging plants. He has arranged lamps and cushions
and covers and books. A Matisse cut-out on the wall. CAROLINE
stands at the door.*

CAROLINE: This is nice. This is really terrific. I don't know why
you kept saying it was vile. [*She goes into the room. WILLIAM
closes the door.*]

WILLIAM: No well...I suppose it was silly...

CAROLINE: It's so stupid, I've never understood it, men always
say sorry, they say it all the time. [*She stands across the room
in her coat. WILLIAM looks up at her.*]

WILLIAM: I wonder...could I get you some brandy?

CAROLINE: What? [*She stares, as if not understanding him.*]

WILLIAM: I have some brandy.

CAROLINE: Oh yes. Okay. [*Pause*]

WILLIAM: I'm really pleased you decided to come back with me.

CAROLINE: What?

WILLIAM: Just feel... [*Pause*] ...a good time.
[*She looks straight across at him.*]

CAROLINE: William, I want to make love to you.

WILLIAM: Yes. [*Pause*] Yes I know. [*He smiles.*] I'm a very lucky
man. [*She is still staring at him. He gestures slightly towards
the bed.*] Why don't we... [*She moves away to the window.*]

CAROLINE: Who do you have living next to you?

WILLIAM: Oh Andrew. He's an Arabic freak. [*He goes to pour two
glasses of brandy from a bottle.*] He's doing his thesis in this
strange little writing. He sits in there, works at it, never looks up.
[*She is looking out of the window.*]

CAROLINE: He sounds really terrific.

WILLIAM: Yes, yes he's nice. His work is his life. [*He hands her a
glass of brandy.*] Here. Here, I drink to your happiness.
[*She looks at him again, in the same way as before. A pause.*]

CAROLINE: William let's get into bed.
[*He moves to the door and turns out one of the lights, leaving
just a bedside light on. She stands quite still at the window, not
moving.*]

WILLIAM: He can speak thirteen dialects. Arabic languages. There
are that many you know. [*The sound of WILLIAM undressing
and getting into bed. We stay on her.*] The thesis he's writing
is all towards a dictionary; it's a dictionary of sixteenth-century

18

Arabic slang. He is really prodigiously clever. [*WILLIAM sitting in bed.*] He is really...a very clever man.

[*There is a pause. Then she turns round and takes her coat off, then walks over and sits on the edge of the bed, with her back to him. She begins to undo her blouse, then pauses quite still. WILLIAM watching her back. She speaks quietly.*]

CAROLINE: I love more than anything to make love to strangers. It's the only time I forget who I am. [*She turns round towards him and starts to undo the remaining buttons. The telephone rings. Her blouse held across her breasts with her hand. She smiles. She looks at him.*] Well?

WILLIAM: What?

CAROLINE: Aren't you going to answer aren't? [*He shakes his head slightly.*] Shall I answer it?

WILLIAM: Sure. If you like.

[*She suddenly reaches right across him for the telephone which is on the table by the bed, still holding her blouse with her hand. She lies across him to answer.*]

CAROLINE: Yes? [*Pause*] Yes? [*Pause*] God. Hello Nicholas.

WILLIAM: What? Who is it?

CAROLINE: No it's fine, it's why I left this number... [*Pause*] What? What for? Oh my god.

WILLIAM: Caroline, will you tell me what's happening...

CAROLINE: No of course not, don't worry...

WILLIAM: What?

CAROLINE: No, no, it's fine, I can be right along... [*She is involuntarily doing up the buttons on her blouse with her spare hand.*] You hold on there, I can be there in ten minutes... [*Pause*] Yeah, I should bloody well hope so. I'll see you in a minute, okay? [*She puts the phone down.*] Well I mean, shit, what can you do about it? Who'd have a brother, that's all I can say. [*She starts to get up and get dressed again.*]

WILLIAM: When did you leave this number?

CAROLINE: Driving under the influence of drink. [*She puts her coat on.*] Anyone who does that, they're just asking for trouble. [*She smiles.*] It should be a principle. Don't drive with long hair. [*She is dressed. She turns and looks at WILLIAM with great kindness.*] Listen, that was a really nice evening. You should be... [*Pause*] Well, you're a very nice man. [*She smiles, looking at him fondly all the time.*]

WILLIAM: Will you...can you try to come back later? [*Pause*]

CAROLINE: Yes, yes, I'll try to. [*Pause*] Yes. Yes of course.


25. INT. WILLIAM'S ROOM/EXT. EARLHAM STREET. NIGHT
*WILLIAM at his window looking down to the street. CAROLINE hurrying along the pavement, her coat tightened against the wind.*

WILLIAM: [*V.O.*] I suppose I waited a week for her phone call. I
    wanted to call her, but I was too proud.

26. INT. NEWS OFFICE. DAY
*Lunchtime in the newsroom. Just a few REPORTERS working,*
*most of the desks deserted. Tape machines, distant typewriters.*
*WILLIAM on the phone at his very messy desk.*
WILLIAM: Hello Caroline. Yeah. Yeah it's William. [*Pause*] He got
    off? Good. That's very good news. [*Pause*] You really did it?
    You gave the police money? Well I was always told that would
    work... [*Pause*] Yes—well I wondered...you know...about
    dinner... [*He smiles.*] Sure we've had dinner, we can have it
    again. [*Pause*] You want me to offer you a different sort of
    evening? Well sure if you tell me what sort of thing you'd like...
    [*Pause*] Well it's just easier, I hardly know you, I don't know
    what sort of evening to choose... [*Pause*] No, I don't think...
    [*Pause*] Well what are you saying? [*Pause*] I think it was good,
    it would be good again.
    [*There is a long pause. He stands his pencil on the desk, lets it*
    *fall. Stands it up again, lets it fall. Then speaks very quietly.*]
    Oh, well right, you have my number. [*Pause*] Yeah all right,
    see you. [*Pause*] Talk to you soon.

27. INT. NEWS OFFICE. DAY
*WILLIAM standing at the agency teleprinter, staring down at the*
*words as they chatter out. Then he rips the sheet out.*
WILLIAM: [*V.O.*] That was the point I should have abandoned it.
    People love chaos. I went on in.

28. INT. HOTEL. RECEPTION ROOM. NIGHT
*A small, dapper LAWYER in a pinstripe suit, very smart.*
LAWYER: This is Keith's first public interview since his highly
    publicized period in jail. Keith wants to talk about the state of
    British prisons, and also tell you something of the future of the
    band. [*A small, private reception room in one of London's*
    *grandest hotels. At one end there are microphones, at the other*
    *a bar. In between, forty members of the PRESS, ranged out in*
    *rows. KEITH on a chair behind the microphones. Behind him,*
    *the other members of the BAND, who are extravagantly dressed.*
    *KEITH is intense, Cockney.*] Keith... [*He steps aside.*]
KEITH: Yeah well right...I think most of you know something...
    how the stuff first got planted in my flat...
    [*WILLIAM, just arrived, at the very back, in his white mac-*
    *kintosh, looking round. KEITH's voice meanwhile.*] I don't
    want to go back over that story...I think most people know it
    pretty well...What I'd like to talk about is what happened
    afterwards...it's not easy...it's not something to put into words.

Basically the whole prison experience is one that's defeating and non-productive all round. [*WILLIAM sitting down next to XAN, a fellow journalist of the same age. XAN has long black hair and a big nose. He wears an overcoat. They whisper.*]

WILLIAM: Xan...

XAN: Good to see you.

WILLIAM: Have I missed anything?

[*XAN shakes his head, still taking notes.*]

XAN: Only just begun.

[*We pick KEITH up in mid-sentence.*]

KEITH: ...there are iniquitous indignities of the system, comparable only to the position inside Soviet Russia...

[*WILLIAM nods quizzically at XAN's shorthand.*]

WILLIAM: Martyr to British Justice?

[*XAN shakes his head.*]

XAN: Cretin Let Out of Jail.


## 29. INT. HOTEL. RECEPTION ROOM. NIGHT

*Later. Chaos. A scrum of FREELOADERS round the bar. The room very noisy. Television cameras, flash floods. XAN trying to get served, WILLIAM looking out across the room.*

XAN: You know, I mean frankly everyone knows it, British prisons are an absolute disgrace...

[*WILLIAM watches as a WOMAN JOURNALIST is nervously introduced to the BAND who are standing in a small formidable group.*]

But I take that story back to my editor, he won't even look up to spit in my face. [*He turns, two whiskies in hand.*] Redbrick journalism, that's what he calls it.

WILLIAM: I know. [*He takes the drink.*] Thanks. [*He smiles.*] They hate our degrees. [*He drinks, watching the room all the time, his conversation automatic.*] And we only mention prisons when there's a rock star. We wouldn't write a word about what it's really like inside...

XAN: What's your interest? This isn't your story.

[*CAROLINE's face glimpsed for a second at the far end of the room, as she slips out the door.*]

WILLIAM: Somebody told me they had a good sound.


## 30. INT. HOTEL. CORRIDOR. NIGHT

*The remains of the reception seen through double doors. The odd WAITER still passing in a white jacket, the last TELEVISION CREW packing up. Through the doors XAN and WILLIAM come out supporting an OLDER JOURNALIST of about fifty-five, in a heavy brown coat. He is having trouble standing up.*

XAN: Right.

WILLIAM: You got him?

XAN: Yeah. Yeah I got him.
  [*The OLDER JOURNALIST slips some way to the floor. As
  he does he holds up his notebook above his head.*]
OLDER JOURNALIST: I got a good story.
XAN: 'Course you have Mike.
OLDER JOURNALIST: I got the most sensational story.
XAN: Yes. Yes of course. Keep moving your legs.
  [*They have him upright. WILLIAM wraps him round XAN's
  shoulder, then hangs back as they begin to move down the
  corridor.*]
WILLIAM: 'Bye Xan.
XAN: 'Bye William.
  [*WILLIAM watches as XAN leads the OLDER JOURNALIST
  off down the corridor.*]
  Come on old friend. I'll find you a taxi. You'll soon be better.
  [*He calls off into the distance.*] Taxi! *The Times*!


31.  INT. HOTEL. CORRIDOR NIGHT
*A long corridor, thickly carpeted. A row of pastel doors. At the
very far end of the corridor WILLIAM is standing in his mackintosh
leaning in slightly, listening at a door as he knocks.*
WILLIAM: Hello. Excuse me. [*He opens the door an inch, then
  calls in, his head still bowed.*] I'm looking for Caroline. [*Pause*]
  Anybody seen her? [*Pause*] Is Caroline there?


32.  HOTEL. BEDROOM. NIGHT
*A shaft of light from the corridor as WILLIAM opens the door. The
light falls across a darkened room in which there are two double
beds, one with a COUPLE lying together, in the other a single MAN.
In between the whole room is devastated: old meals, half-drunk
bottles of bourbon and champagne, drugs, pills, spilt glasses of
water, clothes lying at random, a colour television flickering noise-
lessly in the corner. WILLIAM looks. Absolute silence.*
WILLIAM: Caroline? [*Pause*] Caroline? [*His hand reaching down
  to pull back the sheet which covers the sleeping COUPLE in
  the far bed. He draws it back slightly. The body of the GIRL,
  who is plainly not CAROLINE, doped out, inert. WILLIAM's
  face staring down at her, dispassionate, cool.*] Where are you
  hiding?
  [*CAROLINE's voice from the door.*]
CAROLINE: William... [*He turns. CAROLINE is standing at the
  door, the bathroom door open behind her. She is wearing just
  a shirt, but she looks absolutely fresh and clean.*] Hello. [*She
  looks down, then back across at him, with tenderness.*] I knew
  you'd come back.

## 33. INT. HOTEL. CORRIDOR. NIGHT

*Back outside the room, WILLIAM sitting, head in hands, on a Regency banquette in the corner. CAROLINE in a patterned dress and boots standing opposite.*

CAROLINE: Come on William, I don't understand it. What's all the grief? What have I done wrong? [*Pause*] Why do you think... you've barely spent an evening with me, why do you think you're entitled to feel hurt? [*Pause*] Listen, it's none of your business. Whatever I do. I had to change jobs. These are the people that I have to work with. Sometimes I stay with them. Well that's all right. [*Pause*] I don't see what difference that would make to our evening. [*She kneels down opposite him.*] I really want to see you. [*A long pause. Then he looks up.*] Let's move it, okay?

## 34. INT. HOTEL. STAIRS. NIGHT

*WILLIAM and CAROLINE coming down the stairs together. CAROLINE is laughing and shaking her head, very cheerful.*

CAROLINE: God, well William I can't believe it...

WILLIAM: Why didn't you call me?

CAROLINE: What did you say? [*They disappear round the corner. We just catch the last words as they've gone.*]

WILLIAM: Those people looked really ghastly.

CAROLINE: Yeah. I know. I never take drugs.

## 35. INT. HOTEL. STAIRS. NIGHT

*Further down the stairs, CAROLINE reaches out and lightly stops WILLIAM who is walking ahead.*

CAROLINE: I'd like to take you... I'd like to show you something. I'm really pleased. I've done something good.

## 36. INT. BAND'S OFFICES. NIGHT

*A wall of what turns out to be the BAND's offices. A series of beautiful black-and-white slides, projected. First, a bedroom; a man lying in the bed, a woman with her naked back to us.*

CAROLINE: Here. Look. This is the series. They were taken in a brothel. These are my best. [*The shot held, then changed to a woman standing naked at a basin in an empty room.*] What to you think?

WILLIAM: Yes. They're terrific. [*A girl standing in a G-string next to a man looking into a mirror.*] I didn't know they had them.

CAROLINE: What, brothels? Of course. [*A group of women sitting together on the sofa in their dressing-gowns.*] The band is going to use this lot as projections. Part of their stage show.

WILLIAM: Ah right, I see. [*Another shot of the sofa.*]

CAROLINE: You mean you didn't know there were brothels in London?

23

WILLIAM: Somehow I thought...it's such a strange idea. [*Closer on the sofa.*]

CAROLINE: You should go. They're wonderful places. I know the addresses, I could soon fix you up.

WILLIAM: Well I would rather... [*Another slide.*]

CAROLINE: I can't tell you the trouble I had with the women. Getting them all to come in at once. They're all freaked out, all over London. I had to hire a couple of taxis and go round and literally shake them out of bed. [*A couple more go by, flicking on quicker, as if rejected.*] I tell you I wouldn't like to do it for a living. Organizing that lot. [*A single whore on a sofa, holding her dressing-gown open. She is naked underneath.*] Can you imagine? With a woman photographer. [*Another whore, close.*] That was the best part. [*A long pause.*] When they agreed. [*Then she turns the light on. She picks up a camera and takes a photograph of him, without moving from where she is sitting.*] I'm a very, very good photographer. Didn't you think so? Aren't they very good? [*She gets up to turn the main lights on in the room. WILLIAM stays sitting at a glass-topped desk watching her.*]

WILLIAM: What else is it the band has you doing for them?

CAROLINE: Helping. Being around.
[*WILLIAM smiles.*]

WILLIAM: Are the band pleased? Do they like the photographs? [*She turns at the door.*]

CAROLINE: Good Lord William, I suppose I should ask.

## 37. INT. BAND'S OFFICES. NIGHT

*WILLIAM sitting now in the main secretary's office, which has smaller executive offices going off it. It is very smart in leather and glass, with photos of the BAND and posters of their tours on its walls. CAROLINE is going from room to room collecting paper plates, plastic forks, to go with the salt beef sandwiches and coleslaw which are in greaseproof paper in front of WILLIAM. She talks as she goes.*

WILLIAM: Somebody told me you'd been sacked from the gallery.

CAROLINE: Yeah I committed an error of taste. I ran off fifty-three lithographs. That was three more than the gallery knew. [*She shrugs in the light from a far room.*] I figured what the hell? It's all a commodity. The market's rigged. What difference does it make? [*She smiles as she returns. She has champagne from the executive fridge, which is crammed with bottle of it.*] Of course the point is they like to do the rigging. Nobody else. I'd broken the rules.

WILLIAM: Well in a way you were making a protest.
[*She stops in mid-action and looks at him.*]

CAROLINE: No William. No. I was ripping them off.

## 38. INT. BAND'S OFFICES. NIGHT

*Later. CAROLINE sitting cross-legged on top of one of the desks,
the champagne beside her. WILLIAM drinking from a paper cup.
Their food gone.*

CAROLINE: I had a strange Russian sort of mother. She was hysterical. She made no sense. [*Pause*]. When her family came out
of Russia, they lived for a while at the Savoy. All I've been told
is...they ate so disgustingly the management insisted they lunch
behind screens. That was really...when it came down to it...that
was really their great claim to fame. [*They smile.*] I had no
childhood; Russians don't understand it, they expect you to be
adults from the age of five. I had no father, somewhere we'd
lost him...

WILLIAM: What about your brother? [*She looks at him. Impen-
etrable.*]

CAROLINE: My brother? He's fine.

## 39. INT. BAND'S OFFICES. NIGHT

*They stand in the doorway of the BAND's offices, opposite each
other, close. They are looking at one another. One light is on in the
offices beyond. The corridor is dark.*

WILLIAM: Caroline...I wonder...I'd like you to come home with me.

CAROLINE: Yes, well I shall. [*She smiles.*] I'm on my way. [*Pause*]
I'm afraid...I like it to be easy. I know it's unfair. It's a weakness of mine. [*Pause*] If only you could look...as if it mattered
less to you... [*She turns the light out. Darkness.*] If it just
mattered less to you, then you'd be fine.

## 40. INT. WILLIAM'S ROOM. NIGHT

*CAROLINE in close-up, her hair down, her face on the bedcover.
They are lying sideways across the bed. We are very close.*

CAROLINE: You have that look. I really can't kiss you. When you
have that look, it freezes me up.

WILLIAM: What sort of look?

CAROLINE: The look that says 'help me'. I'm sorry. I can't.

## 41. INT. WILLIAM'S ROOM. NIGHT

*WILLIAM is very angry. He is standing up, trying to hold it back.
CAROLINE sits silently in the corner, her legs tucked up under her,
deep in the armchair.*

WILLIAM: Caroline come on, I mean, God, this is stupid. How can
you do this? This is just mad. [*Pause*] I mean for God's sake
you said you'd come home with me. Then when you get here
you simply freak out. I mean, come on, do you think about my
feelings? I mean, Jesus Christ, will you give me a break?
[*Pause. Then she speaks very quietly.*]

CAROLINE: I know. [*Pause*] It's stupid. I ask too much of you.

[*She looks at him, the same level look we have seen before.*]
I'm very frightened. [*Pause*] I'm in love with you.

## 42. INT. WILLIAM'S ROOM. NIGHT
*WILLIAM's face. CAROLINE's face. The Matisse print above the bed. Nothing moves.*
WILLIAM: [*V.O.*] Oh God. Yes. That was Caroline. [*Pause*] She was always ready. One more trick up her sleeve.

## 43. INT. WILLIAM'S ROOM. NIGHT
*CAROLINE rocking with grief and joy in WILLIAM's arms. The tears are pouring down her face. They hold each other tight.*
CAROLINE: Oh God Jesus William I love you. You're the only man who's ever been kind. You're the first friend...the first friend I've trusted. God how I love you. [*She takes his head in her hands and looks at him.*] You are my friend.

## 44. INT. WILLIAM'S ROOM. NIGHT
*Their faces lying serenely together on the pillow, lit only by the street lights from outside. WILLIAM's eyes are closed. CAROLINE's open. They lie still in the bed.*
CAROLINE: William. [*Pause*] William. [*Pause*] I'm ready for some cocoa. [*He makes a small move.*] You stay. I'll make it.
WILLIAM: Good. Good and strong.
[*CAROLINE throws the cover back. She is fully dressed. She gets out of bed and goes to the door, WILLIAM watching.*]
WILLIAM: [*V.O.*] It was certainly something unusual. [*The door opening. The hall light coming on.*] But it wasn't something I'd see catching on.

## 45. INT. ANDREW'S ROOM. NIGHT
*ANDREW is sitting in bed, naked to the waist, reading a very large book. WILLIAM and CAROLINE come in.*
WILLIAM: Andrew I'd like you to meet Caroline.
ANDREW: Hallo.
CAROLINE: How are you?
WILLIAM: Andrew. Caroline. [*They stand smiling a moment.*]
CAROLINE: I've been cooking. I've made enough for all of us.
ANDREW: Good. Terrific.
CAROLINE: Cocoa. Sausage. And eggs.

## 46. INT. ANDREW'S ROOM. NIGHT
*The three of them feasting on sausages and fried eggs, drinking cocoa. ANDREW is still in bed. CAROLINE in a chair and WILLIAM at ANDREW's work-table. They are all smiling and talking, eating eagerly.*
WILLIAM: [*V.O.*] I certainly remember that evening I was happy. It was certainly the weirdest night I've ever known.

ANDREW: I used to feel some sort of shame in a way.
CAROLINE: Why?
ANDREW: Just because it's odd to like anything so much.
CAROLINE: Why be ashamed?
WILLIAM: I think you're lucky.
ANDREW: Well I admit I don't feel it any more.
WILLIAM: I think what you are is some sort of ideal. Andrew needs
    nothing. Just his work and that's all. I came in here...
ANDREW: Yes, well, we've heard this...
WILLIAM: A complete Indian dinner untouched on the floor. It
    had been there for thirty-six hours...
ANDREW: Bollocks.
WILLIAM: Yes well, sure. That's what you say.
    [*They smile.*]
WILLIAM: [*V.O.*] We sat round talking. It became very easy.
    [*CAROLINE's face smiling as she watches the other two talking,
    unaware.*] We were always closest when someone else was there.

## 47.  INT. ANDREW'S ROOM. NIGHT
*WILLIAM on his feet at the centre of the room, the others watching.
We join in mid-speech.*
WILLIAM: ...Do you know what I think is the great sin of the
    world? Surely, it's caring what anyone else thinks. We ought to
    be able...my God, it should be easy...we ought to be sure
    enough just to be ourselves. [*He smiles round the room. The
    others smile back. CAROLINE looks down, like a mother
    embarrassed by her too-brilliant child.*]
WILLIAM: [*V.O.*] Yes. I remember. I was very happy. I was very
    flattered. I felt I was loved.

## 48.  BLACK SCREEN.
WILLIAM: [*V.O.*]  So it began, that very strange summer...

## 49.  EXT. STREET. DAY
*Notting Hill. A London bus going by, WILLIAM getting off as it
moves, then walking down the road.*
WILLIAM: [*V.O.*] Caroline said the best of her life...

## 50.  EXT. STREET. DAY
*WILLIAM standing on the pavement outside a terraced house in
Notting Hill. He has just rung one of the eight bells.*
WILLIAM: [*V.O.*] I lost my judgement, I had no opinions... [*He
    steps back and looks up to the first floor window.*] Slowly...
    oddly... [*Standing at the window, a bearded YOUNG MAN
    wearing blue jeans, nothing else, gazing ahead.*] I lost my eyes.

51.  INT. CHUEN CHANG KU. DAY
*An enormous Cantonese restaurant in Wardour Street. CAROLINE*
*and WILLIAM standing together waiting to be seated.*
WILLIAM: [*V.O.*] It wasn't a question of actually deceiving me, she
    told me everything, that's what was strange.


52.  INT. CHUEN CHANG KU. DAY
*CAROLINE sitting across the table from WILLIAM. Plain white*
*cloth, the simplest china. They have a plate of fried dumplings which*
*they dip in sauce with their chopsticks.*
CAROLINE: So I had to say to him, we had a good night together,
    why can't we leave it, why talk about love? [*She smiles.*]
    People seem to want to drag you down with them. Why can no
    one be content with a night? When it's good? [*She smiles.*] I
    don't know William, I don't understand it... [*She reaches across*
    *for his hand.*] I'm very grateful I know you, that's all.


53.  INT. CHUEN CHANG KU. DAY
*CAROLINE looking up as the WAITER brings a whole carp in chilli*
*and black bean sauce. It is set down.*
WILLIAM: [*V.O.*] She used to talk to me as if I were impartial. Did
    she never notice she hurt me as well?


54.  INT. NEWS OFFICE. DAY
*At the very far entrance to the enormous room, CAROLINE sitting*
*down in a single chair, smiling up at an OFFICE BOY.*
CAROLINE: No, I'm fine thank you, I'll just wait here. [*The*
    *OFFICE BOY passes frame, turns back uncertain.*] Please don't
    disturb him. I'm actually fine.


53.  INT. NEWS OFFICE. DAY
*At the other end WILLIAM is working at his desk. The whole room*
*is at its busiest, phones ringing, copy going back and forth, people*
*calling across desks. WILLIAM in shirtsleeves, a tie loosely round*
*his neck, totally absorbed in a pile of cuttings.*
WILLIAM: [*V.O.*] Of all the odd things, the one that amazed me,
    she used to come and watch me, not tell me she was there.
    [*STIEVEL calls across from his big desk in the corner.*]
STIEVEL: Hey William, have you got British Leyland?
WILLIAM: Yeah, I have it. Just hold it a mo. [*XAN comes by,*
    *dropping copy on his desk.*]
XAN: Your feature.
WILLIAM: Yes. Thanks. I'll do it. [*He looks up.*] Just leave it
    under all the rest of that stuff. [*He stands up, still totally*
    *absorbed, still reading and walks across the room.*]
WILLIAM: [*V.O.*] She used to say afterwards she'd never desired
    anyone as much as she desired me when I didn't know.

[*He stops, pausing, as if he knew he was being watched. He turns back towards us. We see the chair, now vacated, and just behind it a glimpse of CAROLINE's coat as the door swings shut.*]

56. INT. WILLIAM'S ROOM. NIGHT
*WILLIAM and CAROLINE lying apart on the bed, he looking up to the ceiling, she curled foetally beside him. They are both fully clothed.*
WILLIAM: Please... [*Pause*] Please. [*Pause*] Couldn't you just try? [*Pause*]
CAROLINE: William...I tell you...it's my experience... [*Pause*] in these matters trying doesn't help.

57. INT. WILLIAM'S FLAT. NIGHT
*WILLIAM lying in the bed. CAROLINE sitting on the side of the bed, with a book.*
CAROLINE: This is a long one, all right? [*WILLIAM smiles as she turns back to read.*] 'In Memory of W.B. Yeats'. [*Pause*]
        He disappeared in the dead of winter:
        The brooks were frozen, the airports almost deserted,
        And snow disfigured the public statues...
[*WILLIAM's voice comes over her as she reads.*]
WILLIAM: [*V.O.*] Always implicit there was always the promise, if I held on, the moment would come...

58. INT. WILLIAM'S FLAT. NIGHT
*CAROLINE sitting in the armchair in dead of night, reading quietly, as WILLIAM sleeps. As if she is watching over him.*
WILLIAM: [*V.O.*] All I had to do was to keep my faith with her, keep on trusting her, then we'd be fine.

59. EXT. COUNCIL FLATS. DAY
*WILLIAM talking across a balcony to a WOMAN who is standing in the doorway of a council flat. She is wearing a silver catsuit.*
WILLIAM: [*V.O.*] I spent that summer as a general reporter, interviews, diary pieces, foot in the door...
WILLIAM: Do you think your husband will ever come back to you? [*The WOMAN smiles and begins to answer.*]
WILLIAM: [*V.O.*] Then I ascended to features for a while.

60. EXT. STREET. DAY
*Outside the block of flats. A telephone box in the foreground of the shot. WILLIAM coming out of the main entrance, seeming to ignore the box.*
WILLIAM: [*V.O.*] Most of my time I spent avoiding coinboxes. Every coinbox became a sort of lure.

## 61. INT. TELEPHONE BOX. DAY
*WILLIAM putting tuppence in.*
WILLIAM: [*V.O.*] Whenever she answered I sensed her disappointment. Oh Christ...
  [*WILLIAM speaks with false cheerfulness.*]
  Hello.
WILLIAM: [*V.O.*] ...He's helpless again.


## 62 INT. CAROLINE'S FLAT. NIGHT
*Almost pitch darkness. Just the slightest streak of light falling across CAROLINE's cheek. That is all you can see. WILLIAM's voice on the telephone to her.*
WILLIAM: Caroline... [*Pause*] Caroline... [*Pause*] I just had to ring you. It's awful. I'm sorry. I'm in trouble. You know... [*A pause. A slight movement from CAROLINE.*] I'm so desperate... [*Pause*] I really can't tell you... [*Pause. He is beginning to cry at the other end. CAROLINE's shape does not move.*] I'm just sorry...I need you. You know. [*A pause. He cries.*] I'm sorry Caroline. Jesus. I'm sorry... [*CAROLINE does not move.*]
CAROLINE: It's all right. You must go back to bed. [*She reaches away out of frame. The phone being put down. Her face passing back across the light as she lies down. Silence. Darkness.*]
WILLIAM: [*V.O.*] I never understood why she wouldn't console me. I never understood it. I never shall.


## 63. INT. PHOTO LIBRARY. DAY
*WILLIAM standing at a filing cabinet in the photo and cuttings library. There is one complete wall of green filing cabinets, and at the back of the room there is a sloping glass roof. Morning light. XAN is coming through the door.*
WILLIAM: Hallo Xan.
XAN: How are you?
WILLIAM: What are you up to?
XAN: Middle-class agony. A column of my own... [*He pulls open a filing cabinet drawer.*] How inflation hits the middle class hardest. The editor feels it's a very good idea... [*WILLIAM takes a file and moves away to a table to sit down. XAN takes a tracksuit which has somehow been left in the filing drawer and puts it on top of the cabinets without remark.*] How the working class keep stealing their handbags. How they have to wait so long for a train...
WILLIAM: How the smell of curry drifts into their gardens? [*XAN turns, file in hand.*]
XAN: No. Not quite. We're not going that far. [*He comes to sit down opposite WILLIAM and starts turning the pages of the file.*] We aim for a tone of modest self-righteousness. All decent people getting a bad deal. Always getting mugged at

Valencia airport; how they can't even get a plumber any more. [*He has begun to copy out a clipping into his notebook.*]

WILLIAM: Why do we do it? It's all so dishonest. I've come to feel... [*Pause*] No I can't say. [*XAN goes on writing without looking up.*]

XAN: I only write to claim the expenses. It's my expenses they should publish I feel. That's where my wizardry is fully extend- ed. If I could write as I fiddle, I'd be Mencken, I'm sure. [*WILLIAM is staring at him.*]

WILLIAM: I was talking to someone...she was saying if I felt as I do...the only honest thing would be to confront them. [*XAN doesn't look up.*]

XAN: Yeah. Well remind me, I'd like to be there.

64. INT. NEWSPAPER OFFICES. CONFERENCE ROOM. DAY
*Editorial conference. STIEVEL sitting down at the head of the plastic-topped table in the undecorated room. Twelve JOURNAL-ISTS sitting down around the table, papers and newspapers in front of them, most of them reading, smoking and talking at once. MISS COLLINS passing round with feature lists.*

STIEVEL: Right everyone. Our morning conference. What do we have to set the world on its ear?
[*MISS COLLINS handing him his list.*]

MISS COLLINS: The Queen's in Moose-Jaw.

STIEVEL: Thank you Janice. Right. Round the table. Do we have any more? [*As they being to go round the table, one by one, reading out their plans, WILLIAM's voice over comes in.*]

WILLIAM: [*V.O.*] I see in retrospect everything I did then, every- thing I said was trying to please her.

65. INT. NEWSPAPER OFFICES. CONFERENCE ROOM. DAY
*WILLIAM's turn.*

WILLIAM: Yes well. I can talk about football, talk about film stars... probably shall. But I do wonder why we never spend a confer- ence asking ourselves why we do this job at all.
[*STIEVEL looks up to MISS COLLINS.*]

STIEVEL: Can we have some more coffee?

XAN: Black.

STIEVEL: With sugar.
[*WILLIAM still staring down the table at STIEVEL.*]

WILLIAM: Why we go on every day producing something we know in our hearts to be poor. [*Pause*]

STIEVEL: Now look...

WILLIAM: Listen I don't...I can't claim to be different. I'm just as guilty as anyone here. But I have got tired of living with the feeling that we all end up writing less well than we can. [*Pause*] I came here, I'd worked in Wolverhampton...by no means, not

31

a very good job. But at least there was no special pressure... you never felt you had to level everything down. I mean at this paper we all promote the fiction of nothing very difficult for the people out there. The British public is assumed to be stupid, and in a way that suits us all fine. That's what we offer as our permanent excuse for not actually doing the job very well. [*Pause*] Well I can only tell you, I walk down Fleet Street, I look, I go into the bars. There you'll find...the retreat into alcohol...the smell of bad conscience heavy in the air. [*Pause*] Why do journalists all become cynics? Is it really the things that they see? Isn't it more likely...the cause of their unhappiness...is something to do with a loss in themselves? [*He looks round. Silence.*] I dread a lifetime randomly producing something which we all distrust and despise. I dread the effects on my person of a lifetime given over to royalty and dogs. If we who work here can't believe in it, how the hell can the people out here? [*A pause. STIEVEL looks at him. WILLIAM anticipates his non-existent reply.*] All right. Yes. I know it. I'm sorry. [*Pause*] Listen. Excuse me. I'm afraid I must go.

## 66. INT. NEWSPAPER OFFICES. DAY

*A long tracking shot as WILLIAM and XAN come through the newsroom. XAN exultant. WILLIAM grim.*

XAN: Hey that was great. You really did it. I never thought you'd do it. That was really great. [*He puts his arm round WILLIAM who doesn't stop.*] That was terrific. You just laid it out there. [*He punches WILLIAM lightly on the arm.*] Alcohol. Wow. Hit them where it hurts.

[*XAN disappears into the next office. WILLIAM goes on.*]

WILLIAM: [*V.O.*] I wasn't speaking to anyone present. I was ashamed. I was speaking to her.

## 67. INT. BAND'S OFFICES. NIGHT

*The BAND's offices. Deserted except for CAROLINE who is clearing up her desk, and WILLIAM who is sitting in a hard chair on the other side of the room. CAROLINE is extremely angry as she moves about the office. WILLIAM is miserable.*

CAROLINE: So what do you want? D'you want to be congratulated? Is that it? Come on William are you out of your mind?

WILLIAM: No I'm not...all I'm saying is, well it sound stupid...all I think is I may have done some good. [*He looks across at her.*] Well look for Christ's sake, it's you who encouraged me, it's you who's always saying what an awful rag it is...

CAROLINE: Yes. Right. Good. So you told them. Why do you expect me to praise you as well?

[*He suddenly begins to whine.*]

WILLIAM: Come on Caroline, I can't be expected to...

32

CAROLINE: You told me excited...expecting...why did you come
in here with a smile on your face? [*She turns at the filing
cabinet.*] I never understand it, you say you're independent.
You say you're a person who will stand on his own. Yet whenever you do something virtuous, you seem to think you're
entitled to come to me and collect some reward. [*A pause.
She is hysterical, on the verge of tears. She suddenly spits out
her words with great violence.*] Well that sort of weakness
disgusts me. Do what you have to. Be your own man.
[*WILLIAM looks at her sharply.*]

68. INT. ANDREW'S ROOM. NIGHT
*A poker school. ANDREW's table has been cleared and set in the
middle of the room. The players are pooled under the Anglepoise.
Everyone in shirtsleeves, smoking cigarettes, drinking very cold beer.
The game is seriously played. WILLIAM, ANDREW, XAN and
ROBERT, a self-consciously good-looking blond young man of
about twenty-five who smokes cheroots. ANDREW quietly turns
his hand down.*
ANDREW: Fold [*XAN, already out, smiles slightly at him.*]
WILLIAM: Do I have it?
ROBERT: No. I'll raise you two bob.
WILLIAM: I'll cover that. Raise you again. [*He pushes a pile of
coins forward. ROBERT looks at it, then matches it.*]
ROBERT: See that. Raise you a pound.
WILLIAM: I'll see you.
[*ROBERT turns his hand over.*]
ROBERT: Queens and sixes.
WILLIAM: Aces and fours. [*He smiles.*] Thanks very much.
[*WILLIAM pulls the money towards him, then starts to shuffle.
ROBERT lights a cheroot, then sits back, his hands behind his
head.*]
ROBERT: Xan has been telling me about your life here. Apparently
you've been seeing an old friend of mine. [*WILLIAM smiles,
carries on shuffling.*] All I can hope is you handle her better.
I don't know anyone who held her for long.
[*WILLIAM slides the pack across to ANDREW.*]
WILLIAM: Andrew can you cut? [*Then he looks straight across at
ROBERT.*] She's been a good friend to me.
ROBERT: Oh yes I'm sure. She is. For a time. [*He smiles.*] Every-
one always used to say she was ruthless. But I never minded.
She was so good in bed.
[*WILLIAM takes the cards back, absolutely cool. Then speaks
very quietly.*]
WILLIAM: Well I don't know. Who can judge people? [*He looks
round.*] Why don't we play for a bit more this time?

33

## 69. INT. DANCE CENTRE. DAY

*WILLIAM coming up the stairs at the Dance Centre.*

WILLIAM: [*V.O.*] And so it was, later in the summer, she dis-
appeared completely. She couldn't be found. I think in all she
was gone for a fortnight. Eventually she called me. She'd been
on her own.

## 70. INT. DANCE CENTRE. DAY

*CAROLINE sitting on a chair in leotards, her lunch of yoghurt
beside her. The other DANCERS moving across the room with the
rehearsal PIANIST to go out to their lunch, talking as they go.
WILLIAM walking into the room.*

WILLIAM: [*V.O.*] She was in training. She'd joined a small dance
troupe. Dance and drama. A mixture of the two.
[*CAROLINE is talking.*]

CAROLINE: I'm really pleased. I'd forgotten the discipline.

WILLIAM: What happened to the last job?

CAROLINE: Oh I don't know. [*She turns towards an unseen
mirror as she replaces a grip in her hair.*] I was very hurt. Some
work was rejected. I'd had enough. I wanted to go.
[*WILLIAM looks at her.*]

WILLIAM: I wish you'd rung me. I'd like to have helped you...

CAROLINE: Why would you help me? I'm absolutely fine.

## 71. INT. DANCE CENTRE. DAY

*Four GIRLS performing to some stark Debussy, played at the piano.
A CHOREOGRAPHER walking around the GIRLS. WILLIAM
watching from the rail.*

WILLIAM: [*V.O.*] I don't have to tell you. She looked a great
dancer. [*CAROLINE's face as she dances.*] I was utterly frust-
rated. I put the knife in.

## 72. INT. CAROLINE'S FLAT. NIGHT

*For the first time we see CAROLINE's home. A long oblong room,
it gives the impression of being nine-tenths floor because of the lack
of clutter, and the deeply-stained shiny floorboards. Otherwise,
there are some patterned hangings and a wall of books. CAROLINE
sitting on the floor, WILLIAM with his back to the mirror over the
large fireplace.*

WILLIAM: You must forgive me. I came to tell you. I don't want
to see you. I think we should stop. [*Pause*] I don't know what
role I'm meant to be serving. You never use me. You just want
me there. [*Pause*] If only you could make some movement
towards me... [*Pause*] Touch me. [*Pause*] I crave it I'm afraid.

## 73. INT. CAROLINE'S FLAT. NIGHT

*CAROLINE's face as she turns away to light a cigarette.*

34

WILLIAM: [*V.O.*] It took a long time. It was mostly silence. Whatever I said, I couldn't make her fight.

74. INT. CAROLINE'S FLAT. NIGHT
*CAROLINE smoking a cigarette, WILLIAM in front of her.*
WILLIAM: Look you don't know what people say of you. People say to me you're a cold-hearted bitch. Everyone hates you, they find it offensive...people resent it...the way you're so sure. There's something about it, it puts people's backs up...
CAROLINE: Well thank you, yes, I must bear it in mind. [*She is quite level, absolutely without sarcasm.*]
WILLIAM: Don't you understand, don't you see what I'm saying, it's me who sticks up for you, it's me who stays loyal...
CAROLINE: Yes. Yes I see. And you want a reward?
WILLIAM: No I'm just saying...
CAROLINE: It must be very hard for you. [*Pause*] Yes it's unjust. [*Pause*] One hell of a world.

75. INT. CAROLINE'S FLAT. NIGHT
*WILLIAM sitting silent on his chair.*
WILLIAM: [*V.O.*] I felt disappointed, it wasn't what I wanted, I'd come for hysterics and loss of control...

76. INT. CAROLINE'S FLAT. NIGHT
*They stand opposite each other at the door jamb. The door is open to the landing beyond.*
CAROLINE: Well that's it. You better go now. [*She leans across and kisses his cheek.*] I never loved anyone...I only love you.

77. EXT. STREET. NOTTING HILL. NIGHT
*The house seen from outside. Through the first-floor windows we watch CAROLINE moving about, clearing up coffee cups, ashtrays, apparently impervious.*
WILLIAM: [*V.O.*] Well there it was. I'd done what I came to. I started to watch her, but it came on to rain.

78. INT. ANDREW'S ROOM. NIGHT
*WILLIAM coming in, in his wet mackintosh. ANDREW, as ever, at work at his desk, the Anglepoise on. He looks up.*
WILLIAM: Andrew.
ANDREW: Hey. You look pretty gloomy.
WILLIAM: No. No I'm not. I'm just whacked that's all. [*He smiles, takes a book from his pocket, gives it to ANDREW.*] I happened to see this. It's a first edition...
ANDREW: Browning. Terrific. Thanks very much. [*He smiles at WILLIAM, still holding his pen. WILLIAM stands.*]
WILLIAM: Hey listen, I was wondering, can we go to a movie?

There's one with Carol Lombard which I haven't seen...

ANDREW: Oh good, well yes, I mean I'd really like to. The problem is just...I've a friend coming round. [*Pause*] Perhaps you would like to...

WILLIAM: No, no I wouldn't... [*Pause*]]

ANDREW: I met her last Thursday. We just got engaged. [*He smiles.*] I hope at least you'll hang on to meet her. She's very nice. She works in my field.


## 79. INT. WILLIAM'S ROOM. NIGHT

*WILLIAM coming in the door of his room. His earlier attempts at decency have now collapsed. The room looks like a pigsty again. The eiderdown is on the floor. He stands.*

WILLIAM: [*V.O.*] I could see the future. I was inconsolable. I felt I'd been challenged. And utterly failed.


## 80. INT. COMMONWEALTH HOUSE. DAY

*WILLIAM coming up a very grand staircase in the company of a large group of REPORTERS.*

WILLIAM: [*V.O.*] I then remember little of what happened. I know I was listless, I was bored and depressed...


## 81. INT. COMMONWEALTH HOUSE. DAY

*A big press conference. WILLIAM on his feet in a packed room of JOURNALISTS, notebook in hand.*

WILLIAM: Can the Minister tell us anything of the progress of the EEC negotiations, whether the question of agricultural subsidies is coming up for re-consideration and whether our future partners are going to be any less intransigent about the financial contribution the British are going to make once we're inside the Market?

[*A pinstriped MINISTER of about fifty begins to answer in the bray of his class.*]

MINISTER: Well, let me deal with that question in five parts. First let me say of all these inequities, they will be best dealt with when we are inside...

[*WILLIAM sitting down again. STIEVEL is sitting beside him, as WILLIAM sits...*]

WILLIAM: [*V.O.*] I suddenly found myself popular with Stievel. I have the clear feeling he knew. [*STIEVEL leans across to whisper in his ear, then bursts out laughing, like a schoolboy.*] He'd put down my outburst to an unhappy love-life. Now she was gone, he seemed very cheered.


## 82. INT. ANDREW'S ROOM. NIGHT

*The poker school. The same group in the same positions, except ROBERT has gone and been replaced by another similar YOUNG*

MAN. XAN watching WILLIAM deal.

XAN: Has anyone told you? Your friend Caroline. Apparently she's
back with Robert again.

WILLIAM: No. [Pause] Oh really? [Pause] Well I wish him well
with her. [Then he speaks very quietly.] Let's hope he doesn't
turn out to have needs.

83.  EXT. STAGE DOOR. NIGHT

The stage door of a tatty West End theatre, along an alley. An
ACTRESS comes out and embraces WILLIAM. She is wearing a
great deal of make-up.

WILLIAM: [V.O.] I had a series of rather grim girlfriends, some of
them, well, not particularly nice.

84.  INT. WILLIAM'S FLAT STAIRCASE. NIGHT

WILLIAM and the ACTRESS hastening up the brown-painted stairway to his flat.

WILLIAM: [V.O.] I suppose the truth is I badly needed flattery...

85.  INT. WILLIAM'S FLAT. NIGHT

The door closing as WILLIAM and the ACTRESS go into the room.

WILLIAM: [V.O.] Anyone who wanted me, I'd take them in.

86.  INT. WILLIAM'S FLAT. NIGHT

Continuous. We hold on the closed door. There is a pause. Then the
voice over continues.

WILLIAM: [V.O.] It was later in the autumn I started hearing
rumours. Caroline had apparently been getting very thin. Then
they stopped. Then I heard around Christmas, she'd been found
alone in her room.

87.  INT. CAROLINE'S FLAT. DAY

The pictures of the prostitutes and the brothel which have been
printed as black-and-white photos, and left on CAROLINE's desk.
WILLIAM looking through them.

WILLIAM: [V.O.] Apparently she'd sat there, she hadn't eaten.
When they found her she weighed barely seven stone.
[WILLIAM standing alone in the now deserted flat.]
I thought if I go it will only upset her. So I just gave the doctor
a ring.

88.  INT. ANDREW'S ROOM. NIGHT

The only difference is that at the other end of the table, under
another Anglepoise, BARBRA, a pale chubby blonde, now works as
well. WILLIAM sitting at the other side of the room.

WILLIAM: Well they're saying it's just undernourishment. She had
some idea of living on her own. Apparently the worst is...it

makes her hallucinate. [*Pause*] They're not worried. They just
think she's thin. [*Pause*]
ANDREW: I suppose you don't know...does she ever ask for you?
WILLIAM: Yes, I should ask that. I should certainly find out.

## 89. INT. ANDREW'S ROOM. NIGHT
*ANDREW and BARBRA returning to their work as WILLIAM gets*
*up and leaves the room, goes out into the corridor and into his own*
*room.*
WILLIAM: [*V.O.*] I started ringing, I rang in often. I mean I always
rang at least once a week.

## 90. INT. WILLIAM'S ROOM. NIGHT
*WILLIAM lying wide awake in bed at night.*
WILLIAM: [*V.O.*] She began to get better. She put some weight on.
But it counted for nothing. She'd lost her mind.

## 91. INT. EARLS COURT FLAT. DAY
*CAROLINE's mother, MRS ALEXANDER, wearing black, sitting on*
*an ornate gilded chair in a highly decorated but very seedy flat in*
*Earls Court. There is a great deal of gilded furniture and mirrors and*
*lamps which now look neglected and tatty. MRS ALEXANDER is*
*fifty-five, elegant, taut, emotional. WILLIAM sits opposite, uneasy.*
MRS ALEXANDER: You are the boy. She spoke warmly of you.
She was much in love. You were always the one.
[*WILLIAM looks down.*]
WILLIAM: Well...
MRS ALEXANDER: It's all right. There is no accusation. You did
what you had to. You followed your heart.
[*They sit across the room from one another, the darkness com-*
*ing down.*]
WILLIAM: [*V.O.*] Her mother turned out to be very, very stupid. I
spent the evening listening to her talk...
MRS ALEXANDER: I can tell you must be experienceed, you are so
good-looking I'm sure you're pursued. Such looks. Do you find
them a handicap? No, not a handicap. A blessing I suppose.

## 92. INT. EARLS COURT FLAT. EVE
*MRS ALEXANDER in mid-conversation, unceasing.*
MRS ALEXANDER: Of course now she's left me, I have no money,
I've relied on Caroline, I've no money of my own...
WILLIAM: [*V.O.*] All evening I listened, the talk flowed out of her,
nothing would stop it. A life of its own...

## 93. INT. EARLS COURT FLAT. EVE
*Later. The dark almost down. MRS ALEXANDER well warmed to*
*her themes.*

MRS ALEXANDER: The Blacks are now all over this neighbour-
hood, those who aren't Blacks are invariably Jews...it's just no
longer a place for decent people... [*She continues.*]
WILLIAM: [*V.O.*] It all seemed pointless. What good could I do?

94. EXT. SPRINGFIELD. DAY
*Ext. of Springfield Psychiatric Hospital. A splendid façade with an in-
dustrial chimney, lawns in front. WILLIAM walking along the drive.*
WILLIAM: [*V.O.*] Later that winter she transferred to Springfield.
I went to see her.

95. INT. HOSPITAL. LOUNGE. DAY
*The lounge of one of the women's wards at Springfield. CAROLINE
in a velvet T-shirt sitting on one of the armchairs, alone. There are a
number of chairs, a colour TV, some tables with games.*
WILLIAM: [*V.O.*] She was feeling very bad.

96. INT. HOSPITAL. LOUNGE. DAY
*WILLIAM sitting opposite CAROLINE in the otherwise deserted
lounge.*
WILLIAM: I'm sorry. I feel...I let you down badly. I should have
seen you earlier. [*Pause*] I had a feeling...I brought you some
papers. Here. There's something to read. [*Pause*] I hope you
realize...how much we miss you. You must be quick, we need
you back there. [*He gets up and bends down to kiss her, a
little patronizingly, on the forehead.*]

97. INT. HOSPITAL. CORRIDOR. DAY
*The lounge seen from the corridor. We watch WILLIAM and a
DOCTOR walking towards us, talking as they come.*
WILLIAM: [*V.O.*] Of course I suppose if I have to be truthful, part
of me admits to a feeling of relief...
DOCTOR: ...long-term damage, it's too soon to say...
WILLIAM: [*V.O.*] I'd always believed the things that she told me,
everything she'd said about how one should live.
[*He shakes hands at the door, smiling.*]
WILLIAM: Well doctor, I must thank you.
DOCTOR: No, not at all. I'm delighted to help.
[*The two of them walk out of the frame which is now empty.
We stare at the room beyond.*]
WILLIAM: [*V.O.*] Now it turned out...well I was grateful...that's
what I felt. Thank God she was mad.
[*There is a pause. Then CAROLINE crosses from the hidden
part of the room and with her back to us moves out of the door
at the very far end of the room.*]

[*Very fast fade.*]

98.   BLACK SCREEN
*Held for two seconds, then:*

99.   EXT. FLEET STREET. DAY
*WILLIAM walking along Fleet Street in the evening rush-hour, one face among five hundred on the pavement. He is older.*
WILLIAM: [*V.O.*] Since that time I haven't done badly, I have a
    family, a very kind wife...

100.   INT. WATERLOO STATION. EVE
*WILLIAM getting on to a crowded commuter train at Waterloo, then reading his paper on the train.*
WILLIAM: [*V.O.*] The paper has been losing circulation, so of
    course we've all had to keep on our toes. That situation has
    been quite interesting...though most of the time I'm chained
    to a desk.

101.   INT. HOUSE. HALL. NIGHT
*WILLIAM coming through the door of his house. A very pleasant, cork-tiled, pine-furnished house full of plants and flowers. His children playing indoors as he comes.*
WILLIAM: [*V.O.*] Laura and I have had some very good times
    together...holidays, parties, evenings at home. Ben is much the
    most active of our children...
    [*We see through to the kitchen where LAURA is preparing
    dinner. She is small and dark, very attractive in blue jeans.*]
    Ellen, the youngest, was born a bit slow.

102.   INT. KITCHEN. NIGHT
*WILLIAM pouring out gin and then tonic into two ice-filled glasses, taking them across to LAURA who is now at the stove. They are talking and smiling.*
WILLIAM: [*V.O.*] We've always tried to keep an open marriage. I
    mean I think a marriage is refreshed by affairs. I wouldn't
    necessarily recommend it to everyone, but if you can do it...
    and not go too far.

103.   INT. SITTING ROOM. NIGHT
*Later. Darker. WILLIAM and LAURA sitting at opposite sides of the room, both quietly reading.*
WILLIAM: [*V.O.*] Obviously Caroline is much with me. I mean it's
    something I shan't ever forget. What I always took to be her
    self-confidence, now seems a way she had of hiding her fears.

104.   INT. CHILD'S BEDROOM. NIGHT
*BEN fast asleep in his bunk. He is five. His face is serene on the pillow.*
40

WILLIAM: [*V.O.*] It breaks my heart that she couldn't reach out to me. If I'd been wiser perhaps I would have known.
[*WILLIAM's face comes into frame as he reaches for the small bedside light in front of BEN. The light goes out. Darkness.*]

## 105. INT. BEDROOM. NIGHT
*WILLIAM and LAURA sitting on opposite sides of the bed, undressing. The warm light of a single bedside lamp.*
WILLIAM: [*V.O.*] If anyone now asks me what I feel about these incidents, I can only tell you what I think for myself.
[*His wife's graceful body as she gets into bed. WILLIAM reaching out to embrace her. Their faces as they kiss. A long pause. They look at each other.*]
Our lives dismay us. We know no comfort. [*Pause*] We have dreams of leaving. Everyone I know.
[*WILLIAM turns away. The camera pulls out. The light is suddenly turned out.*]